PERFORMING PLANTS

Performing Plants

by

WARE T. BUDLONG

—

illustrated by

GRAMBS MILLER

SIMON & SCHUSTER · NEW YORK

The author gratefully acknowledges the assistance given her in the preparation of this book by the Boyce Thompson Institute for Plant Research, Yonkers, New York, and the staff of the New York Botanical Gardens, Bronx, New York.

Text copyright © 1969 by Theodore Budlong
Illustrations copyright © 1969 by Grambs Miller
Published by Simon & Schuster, Inc., Children's Book Division
Rockefeller Center, 630 Fifth Avenue
New York, New York 10020

Second Printing

SBN-671-65042-4 Trade
SBN-671-65043-2 Library
Library of Congress Catalog Card Number: 68–29761
Manufactured in the United States of America

Contents

I

Plants That Perform With You

MEN HAVE USED plants for food ever since our earliest ancestors began to supplement the bounty of the hunt with the fruits—and stems, leaves, and roots—of trees and grasses. Plants have been used in thousands of other ways—in making tools and building shelters, as medicines and in making paper, in dyes, decorations and perfume—since prehistoric times, too. The cultivation of flowers for pleasure is not quite so ancient but extensive parks and gardens were owned by the wealthy Babylonians and Greeks many centuries before the birth of Christ.

Today, gardens can be grown for pleasure by anyone, indoors or out, and they may contain plants that are common, or those that come from places thousands of miles away. While planting and cultivating a garden of any kind is a delightful and rewarding experience, special kinds of gardens that contain plants grown for a specific purpose can provide a fascinating project. A garden of performing plants, of flowers that move, grow, or respond to something in little-known or unusual ways, can be an absorbing, year-round pleasure.

To have a garden of performing plants, you need little more than seeds, soil, and flowerpots or a window-box planter, or, if you are fortunate enough, a small plot of ground. Sunlight, water, and your own curiosity and care will do the rest.

The size and extent of such a garden will depend upon your own interest and adventurousness.

Selection of plants, of course, depends to some extent on the kind of garden you want and the climate where you live. An indoor garden will suit any location. Your plants can be grown in individual flowerpots or in larger rectangular planters. A one-half- to one-inch layer of small pebbles placed in the bottom of the pot or planter will provide proper drainage over which you can place the soil. (Directions for making a terrarium or glass-enclosed planter are given in Chapter III, page 25.)

In warm climates, you can consider an outside garden. And for a change of location, in an area where the winters are cold, use a long planter, an indoor window box, that will stay in a sunny, south-facing window part of the year and can be moved outdoors as the climate permits.

For quicker results, you may want to order some plants instead of starting your whole garden from seeds. Since the plants will vary in height, some ordinary nonperforming plants may be added to complete a design. A low border of small plants will frame the whole effect.

One kind of flower for a garden of performing plants might be the compass plant. In the early 1800's, frontiersmen and hunters on the prairies of the Mississippi Valley discovered a sunflowerlike plant whose leaves indicated the points of the compass. The sturdy leaves of this plant, whose Latin name is *Silphium laciniatum,* grow in such a way that their edges point north and south, while their broad upper and lower surfaces are exposed to the east and west. The seeds of this plant

COMPASS PLANT

are not usually available at all garden supply stores, so check the list on page 88 for nurseries or seed houses where you may order them, as well as seeds of other plant performers.

A better-known plant, *Mimosa pudica,* is so extremely sensitive that it is commonly called the sensitive plant. Perhaps you have touched mimosa leaves and watched them fold gently under your fingers. This plant also folds its leaves at night and opens them again with the approach of daylight. Mimosa will

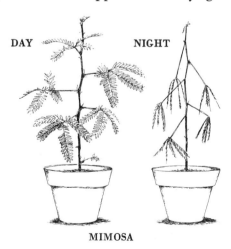

DAY   NIGHT

MIMOSA

9

be mentioned later, in connection with a special experiment.

The obedient plant, *Physostegia virginiana,* is another plant that responds to touch. Its flowers are jointed at the base and you can turn them back and forth as if they worked on tiny ball bearings.

The telegraph plant, *Desmodium gyrans,* regularly per-

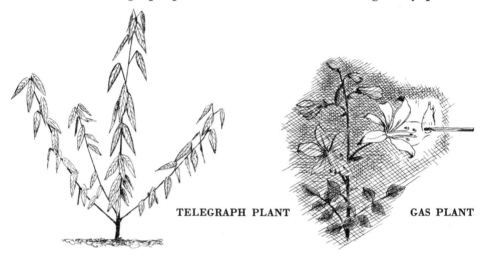

TELEGRAPH PLANT   GAS PLANT

forms on its own, every few minutes. It has small leaflets fitted near the stem end of the larger leaves. These leaflets move up and down like the action of a telegraph key tapping out a message. The leaves of the telegraph plant also change position at night, drooping down with a sleepy look.

A plant that needs cooperation to make its effect is the gas plant, *Dictamnus albus.* On a hot summer evening when the air is still, the gas plant will give off a volatile oil from its flowers. This vapor will flash into flame if you hold a lighted match near the stem. Any such experiment must, of course, be done with extreme caution.

Further choices for a garden of performing plants can be

10

made from many mentioned in other sections of this book. You might want to have an oxalis plant, because it shoots its seeds out with a pistol-shot noise, or rattlesnake iris because when the wind moves the seed pods, the seeds rattle. You might want to include a trumpet flower, to watch the twining action of its tendrils. It was the great English naturalist Charles Darwin, who, observing this action, began his study of the movement of plants.

Aerial plants can be especially attractive, hanging above an indoor garden or hung alone in a window. A most unusual mobile can be made with what are popularly called magic leaves. These are leaves of an air plant, *Kalanchoe pinnata*. The leaves can live detached from the plant, and will form tiny new leaves along their edges. If the plant is suspended in a hanging pot, its leaves will grow in a spiral, turning in small circles inside a larger circle.

These leaves get their food and moisture from the air. But they will grow better with a light spray of water now and then during the indoor heating period of a Northern winter. After some months of enjoying the mobile, you can settle the plantlets in soil and raise a new supply of magic leaves.

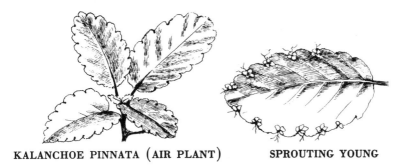

KALANCHOE PINNATA (AIR PLANT)   SPROUTING YOUNG

If you live where the weather is warm most of the year, a

more ambitious project that you may want to try is a floral clock. Certain plants open and close their flowers at definite hours of the day. Thus, if you plan your garden so that the flowers that open or close are in hourly sequence, and in the shape of a clock, you can tell the approximate time by observing their actions.

The eighteenth-century scientist Linnaeus, whose name was actually Carl von Linné, made his own floral clock in Sweden in 1748. When the clock was completed, his friends said they often could tell the time, on entering the garden, from the scent of flowers that marked the hours.

A modern version of this clock, with flowers that suit the section of the country where you live, will make a garden of fascinating activity. Your parents, or your biology teacher, or a garden nursery can help you pick out seeds to plant whose flowers will open and close at different times of the day. Make a rough circle, about 18 inches in diameter, and outside the circle you can sow five or six different kinds of seed, some of which open early in the morning when the sun is fully up, and some which open later in the day or toward the evening.

Choose plants which flower naturally at the same time of the year in your neighborhood. No plant really tells you that it is 7:15 and time to get up. Its habits, though, will be fairly regular, depending upon the amount of light its gets. If you have some success with your floral clock on your first try, you can check next year on some harder-to-get seeds which you can start indoors and transplant outside when the ground is warm.

Listed opposite are some plants whose flowers open and close regularly during a 24-hour cycle. The times noted for their opening or closing are given by Eastern Standard Time, but this may vary considerably under specific local conditions.

PLANTS THAT PERFORM WITH YOU

Time	*Plant*	*Others*
5–6 A.M.	Dwarf morning glories open.	Wild roses open. Pumpkin flowers open.
7–8	Dandelions open.	
8–9	African daisies open.	
9–10	Gentians open. Pumpkin flowers close.	
10–11	Tulips open. California poppies open.	
11–12	Moonflower closes.	
Noon	Morning glories close.	Goatsbeard opens. Chicory opens. Star-of-Bethlehem opens.
4 P.M.	Four-o'clocks open.	
4–5	California poppies close.	
Sunset	Evening primrose opens. Moonflower opens.	
8–9	Day lilies close. Dandelions close.	
9–10	Flowering tobacco opens.	
10–2	Night-blooming cereus opens.	

As a contrast to this carefully designed effect, you might choose a wide corner of an outdoor plot for a walking-plant garden, where the performers will have plenty of room. Wherever you start them, you may be sure they will move off in some other direction. These plants move, apparently, in search of less crowded soil, or water and sunlight.

The walking fern will send out a long narrow frond that touches the ground, takes root and produces a new plant there. It should be started in partial shade and kept well watered.

WALKING FERN

'White clover will travel across the garden, as will wandering Jew. Strawberry plants, which you may have considered only for their blossoms and fruit, are also traveling plants. Start them in their own section of the garden and let them go where they will. You will eventually have an interesting pattern of crisscrossing, traveling plants.

14

WHITE CLOVER

WANDERING JEW

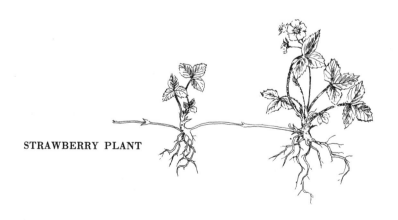

STRAWBERRY PLANT

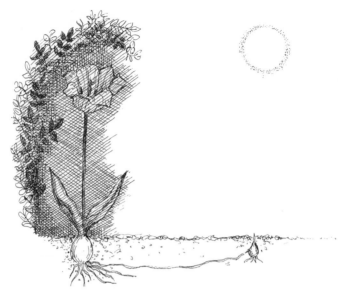

TULIP, MOVING TO A SUNNIER SPOT

Tulips belong in this garden. Have you ever noticed that you may plant tulips in a careful arrangement, and find them appearing the next year in another position? Plant the bulbs in shade, with strong sunlight nearby. You will find they send out shoots and start new bulbs where the sunlight is, gradually transferring food material from the old bulbs to the new and finally appearing in the sun.

As a special performer for the garden, add a plant that leaps. This is the life plant, *Bryophyllum pinnatum.* Its leaves can live separated from the plant, like the magic leaves used in the mobile, with new plants growing from them. Leaves detach themselves from the parent plant, fall to the ground, and start new growth in a new place.

There is always something happening in a garden where the plants make the design.

16

II

Tropisms

PLANTS ARE KNOWN to respond to certain things, such as a touch, or light. These responses are called tropisms. Some responses are slow, and can be observed only by patient watching; others are quick, the plants putting on an effective and immediate performance.

The sensitive plant, *Mimosa pudica,* responds to the touch of a finger. The leaves fold at once. This plant is easy to obtain, usually as seed, at a nearby nursery or by mail. When you test it, touch some of the leaves and leave others open, for contrast.

MIMOSA

The importance of light to flowers is familiar to us from watching the reaction of house plants, such as the geranium that turns its leaves to face the light from a window. You can use a plant's response to light, called heliotropism or phototropism, by persuading a plant to make a deep bow. The directions for doing this are given at the end of the chapter.

The response of a plant to gravity is shown by the fact that all roots grow downward, a reaction called positive geotropism. The action of the stem, always growing up, is called negative geotropism. One example of the response to gravity can be shown by a cut stalk of gladiolus. When placed flat on a table for a few hours, the flowered tip will start to lift upward from the table, showing negative geotropism. You may have noticed that the ends of gladiola stalks are often turned at angles. Because of this sensitive response to gravity, commercial shipments are often made with the flowers standing straight up, so that they won't bend at odd angles.

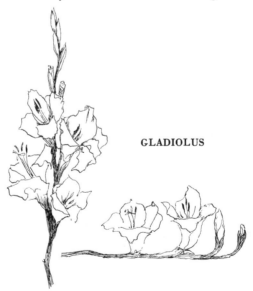

GLADIOLUS

The reaction of plants to chemical substances is wide and familiar. An interesting example is the experiment in growing giant and dwarf plants, which is discussed later in this chapter.

Plants also respond to water and to electric current, and to a source of heat. One of the more recently discovered forms of tropism is magnotropism, or the reaction of plants to the earth's magnetic field.

The ability of plants to move was demonstrated by Charles Darwin. Darwin may be best known for his theory of evolution by natural selection, but he also did great service in studying certain types of plant performance.

Before Darwin's work, carried on in the latter part of the nineteenth century, it was generally believed that plants were distinguished from animals, in part, by not having the power of movement. But Darwin said that plants "acquire and display this power [of movement] only when it is of some advantage to them." And he proved this ability of plants to move, when it was to their advantage to do so, with precise experiments.

He also considered that the powers of plants were more specific than had been believed before. "It is hardly an exaggeration," he wrote, "to say that the tip of the radicle [the root], having the power of directing the movements of the adjoining parts, acts like the brain of one of the lower animals." However you may accept this comparison, you can observe that the root of the plant always goes down, while the stem goes up. This can be demonstrated vividly by turning a partly grown

THE ROOTS OF A BULB PLANTED UPSIDE DOWN
WILL STILL GROW DOWNWARD

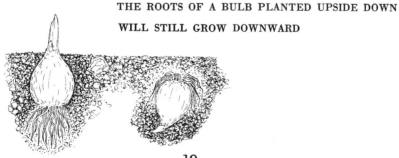

19

plant upside down, and noting that the root and stem will gradually turn to face their normal directions.

Some plants, such as the morning glory, the pea, and the wild honeysuckle, are called twining plants because they have flexible stems and are capable of coiling around a support.

Darwin did many experiments with twining plants, showing their ability to revolve in search of a support, and to coil about the support when they found one. He demonstrated, for example, that if a twining plant or its slender, leafless tendril is put into an inclined or slanting position, it soon bends upward to climb again. And he proved that in twining plants, every part of the shoot or tendril has its own power of independent movement. He illustrated this last point by tying all of a revolving shoot to a stake, except the last two inches at the tip; this small free part continued to revolve.

You can do one of Darwin's experiments for yourself to show the effect of light on a twining plant:

Place a morning-glory plant in a room where the only light comes from a single nearby window. Now, with a pencil and paper, tape measure, and a clock, time the revolutions of a

MORNING GLORY

20

tendril of your plant. Morning glory will make a complete revolution in approximately five and one-half hours, and you can check this. Take your timings at fifteen-minute intervals if possible, or half-hour intervals. Measure the distance covered by the tendril in its revolution each time you check it. You will find that the speed of revolution increases as the plant tip approaches the window light, and slows down as the tip leaves the light. A semicircle away from the light takes about four and one-half hours, while the semicircle toward the light takes only about an hour. When you make the exact timing record for your plant, as you will see, the total time will remain constant. That is, no matter how much faster the tip moves as it goes toward the light, the time for a complete revolution will always be the same.

In a report of recent experiments at Yale University, by Drs. M. J. Jaffe and A. W. Galston, certain characteristics of twining plants were noted: "Plants with flexible stems have evolved various means of supporting their leaves above those of their competitors. Among these devices, and usually classed as their most highly evolved form, are tendrils." The report goes on to define tendrils as flexible, threadlike organs that are sensitive to touch, a response known as thigmotropism. When the tendril touches a supporting object, such as a stake or a strong stem of another plant, it will then coil around it.

"The tendrils of most species are, as they mature, capable of circummutation (curves or ellipses), often in a direction independent of that of the stem. This sweeping through space gives the tendril a better chance to contact a support. When a tendril does touch the support, contact coiling occurs, during which the tendril wraps itself around the support." This report

21

takes up specifically the growth of tendrils and aspects of contact coiling of the Alaska pea plant, and is included in the Bibliography.

Four experiments, easily done at home, follow. In each, a plant, or part of a plant, is induced to perform.

To persuade a plant to make a deep bow, you will use its response to light. You will need a sturdy seedling or partly

1

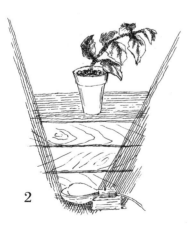

2

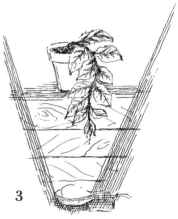

3

grown young plant in a flowerpot. The plant should be tall enough so it can eventually curve over the edge of the pot and down. Place the plant on a box, close to the edge, in a closet. On the floor just below the plant, place a small lamp so that its beam is directed up the side of the box beside the plant. Keep the closet closed, so the only light is from the lamp. Check the plant daily to see if it needs water, and observe what happens. Gradually the plant will curve down toward the light, as shown in the illustration, until finally it is making its bow.

An experiment that takes longer, but has a dramatic effect, is to start with four plants, two geraniums and two chrysanthemums, and turn one geranium and one chrysanthemum into giants and the other two into dwarfs. For this, you will need to buy two chemicals at a garden center or from one of the suppliers listed at the back of the book. For the growth stimulators, you will need Wonder-brel or Gibrel. For dwarfing a plant, you will need Amo-1618 or B-nine. Follow the directions given on the containers for amounts of the chemicals to be added and how often to add them. The geraniums will show good response to the growth stimulator, and the chrysanthemums to the dwarfing chemical. As the plants grow, you can watch the contrast in their sizes.

A quick experiment can be made with the mimosa plant that you watched fold its leaves at your touch. If you can obtain a small quantity of chloroform from your druggist, place the plant in a tight container, with a small quantity of the chloroform in a dish near it. After half an hour, take the plant out. Now it has been anaesthetized and will not respond to your touch. But after a short time, the effect of the chloroform will wear off, and once again the plant will respond to touch.

Another quick experiment shows an interesting slow-motion effect of static electricity on a dandelion puffball, the fluffy round ball you see when a dandelion goes to seed. The silky parachutes of the seeds will appear before the puffball breaks up. Use a plastic comb, which you can charge with static electricity by rubbing it on your hair or against a piece of fur. Hold the puffball near the comb. The seeds will be attracted to the comb. But they will move in slow motion, as compared with sawdust particles, for example, because the parachutes on the seeds provide a drag resistance.

DANDELION SEEDS ARE ATTRACTED BY STATIC ELECTRICITY

III

Carnivorous Plants

CARNIVOROUS, OR MEAT-EATING, plants put on regular performances. They can be tempted to perform with insects, and sometimes with small bits of raw meat.

Some of these plants will live indoors in an open container. Others should have the moist air of a terrarium. They can be found in various areas of the country, growing wild, or can be ordered from suppliers. Though some of the carnivorous plants, such as Venus flytrap and the northern pitcher plant, may do well in an open planter, they will all do better in the humidity of a terrarium. And when you go away for a weekend, all you have to do is water and feed the plants before you leave, and close the top.

Terraria, or terrariums as they are commonly called, are glass cases with glass tops. These may be ordered with the carnivorous plants, or you can make your own easily and cheaply. For a base, use a low wooden box, such as a flat from a nursery, which is used for seedlings and often may be had for the asking. Seal all the cracks with a good waterproof cement, which can be bought at the hardware store. Then paint the box with rot preventative, also from the hardware store. Test the box, to make sure it is watertight. Have five pieces of glass cut at the glazier's or hardware store: two that fit the inside side measurements of your box; two that fit the ends (minus two thicknesses

of glass, so the end pieces will fit inside the side pieces); one for the top, one-half inch larger on all sides than the size of the box, to provide edges for lifting. Run a strip of caulking material around the bottom of the box, close against the sides. Into this material, set the four glass sides firmly. Tape them at the corners with plastic tape. Tape all edges of the glass cover, so there will be no chance of cut fingers when it is lifted off.

The height of the glass sides will depend on the effect you want, or whether you plan to buy some of the taller plants. Pictures in a supplier's catalogue will show the variations of the plants.

One of the most spectacular of the carnivorous plants is the Venus's-flytrap, or as it is commonly called, Venus flytrap. This will grow well in an indoor garden or in a flowerpot.

The leaves are small traps, hinged in the middle. The edges of the leaves are fringed, and on the inside surface of the leaf are very sensitive hairs. These hairs, when touched, trigger the closing of the two sides of the leaf to make the trap, as shown in the drawing.

An insect crawling across the leaf will trigger the action,

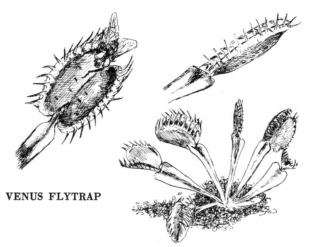

VENUS FLYTRAP

which is swift enough to catch the insect. Then the insect is gradually digested.

When you get some Venus flytrap plants, touch a leaf with a pencil point to see the trap work. Then catch a few flies or ants for your plants. When you have a hamburger, save a tiny bit of uncooked meat to feed your plants.

Butterwort is an insectivorous herb that needs moist air. It will grow in sphagnum moss, or a mixture of peat moss and sand, and should be kept moist. This plant also traps the insects

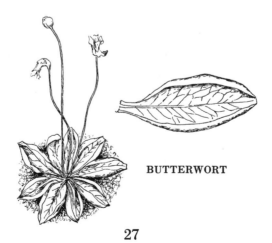

BUTTERWORT

27

that light on the surface of the leaves. These leaves, set in a rosette, secrete a sticky liquid that attracts insects and holds them glued tight after they alight on a leaf. As the insect moves on the leaf, the leaf curls tighter to form a container.

Sundew also likes a damp home but works a bit differently to catch its food. Its leaves end in pads covered with tiny hairs that are tipped with a sticky liquid as well as with an odor that attracts insects. The sticky substance shines in the sunlight, drawing the insects' attention that way, too. When an insect touches a pad and gets trapped in the sticky liquid, the hairs bend toward the center, enclosing the insect and pressing it into the plant's digestive fluids that are secreted by the hairs.

Sundew is well distributed around the country in marshy ground. If you collect some, take along some of the moss around it, or buy peat moss at a garden center or dime store. Keep the sundew in a container with a cover until you set up your terrarium.

When you feed the sundew with insects, chopped meat, or small bits of other protein substance, you can also test the

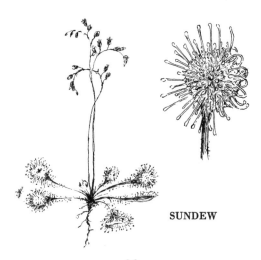

SUNDEW

plant's recognition of protein. Place a very small bit of wood or twist of paper on a leaf. The leaf will respond to the touch and close over this substance—but will soon release it because there is no protein to be found.

Plants of both sundew and Venus flytrap may be ordered by mail. You can also buy seeds, and grow them in a corner of the terrarium, or in a covered glass container, on a medium of sand and peat moss, kept dampened.

There are many varieties of pitcher plants among the carnivorous group, and before ordering them, it's a good plan to decide on the size of your terrarium. You will need a tall one for some of the pitcher plants, or you can order certain plants that do not grow as tall.

Pitcher plants have hollow leaves that will hold water. The plants also produce chemicals that attract insects, drug them when they are caught, and then help to absorb and digest them. Some plants have open pitchers, while others have pitchers with lids. Inside the leaf pitchers are bristles that point down, so when an insect is attracted inside, it is directed toward the bottom and cannot easily crawl out again.

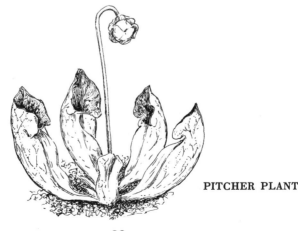

PITCHER PLANT

Northern pitcher plants grow to only about six inches in height and are a good choice for a low terrarium. The parrot pitcher is also low, reaching about the same height.

Some varieties of the Sarracenia pitcher plant are taller. The *Sarracenia rubra* grows to about twenty inches. The hooded trumpet, *Sarracenia minor,* may reach two feet in height.

Dramatic pitcher plants for a tall terrarium case are the huntsman's horn, *Sarracenia flava.* These may grow up to three feet tall, and the cobra lily is equally tall. The cobra lily has pitchers that resemble the head of the snake from which it gets its name. There are even fanglike trailers below the hood which produce a liquid that attracts insects. When insects progress along the "fangs" and reach the opening of the hood, they often slip into the liquid waiting at the bottom of the pitcher. Sometimes they notice the translucent spots on the inside of the hood, which appear to be openings, and in trying to get through

HUNTSMAN'S HORN

these, fall into the liquid. One way or another, enough insects are trapped to provide food.

When the terrarium has been completed and planted with carnivorous plants, settled into a marshy ground, the top should be put on to hold moisture in. It can stay open about an inch, to provide fresh air and prevent moisture from forming on the glass sides. If the glass gets heavily misted, leave the top off for a little while.

Meat-eating plants go right on performing for your amusement, and do a special show for visitors. So remember to take them a fly, an ant, or a bit of raw meat.

I V

Plant Partnerships

SOME PLANTS grow better when special "friends" are close by. Sometimes it is another plant that makes the difference. Sometimes it is an insect that enters into a working partnership with a plant.

The quality of living closely together with another plant or animal with an advantage in this nearness is called *symbiosis*. It is a Greek word that means the state of living together, and modern usage has added the point of benefit. This benefit, strictly speaking, is mutual, working both ways. The two herbs, rosemary and sage, have a stimulating effect on each other's

SAGE   ROSEMARY

growth, for example. But sometimes the nearness assists one plant more than the other.

Roses benefit from the nearness of several other kinds of plant. Mignonette is helpful to roses, and also to parsley. Roses and garlic are mutually beneficial. And marigolds are an important ally of roses, killing the nematode worms—root-knot nematodes—which destroy root cells in the roses. The marigold does this by an excretion from its own roots that is poisonous to the nematode worms.

WILD ROSE   GARLIC

Rachel Carson, in *Silent Spring,* tells the story of roses in a city park in Holland that were in poor condition because of nematodes. Scientists of the Dutch Plant Protection Service recommended that marigolds be planted among the roses. So some rose beds had marigolds added, while others, as controls, were left without marigolds so that the effect of the experiment could be properly judged. The results showed that the control beds of roses were still in poor condition, but where marigolds had been planted the roses flourished.

Herbs have been known for a long time to have the quality of repelling pests. The majority of herbs benefit vegetables, repelling insects that would otherwise attack them.

Some vegetables are good companions to each other. Beans, for example, do well planted near carrots. And beans

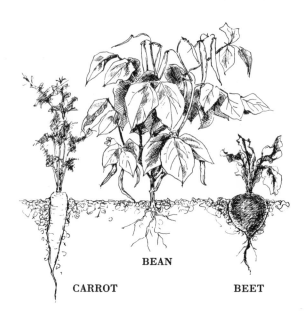

BEAN

CARROT

BEET

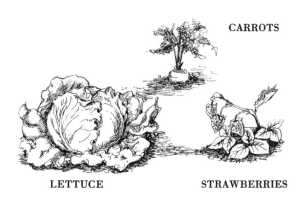

CARROTS

LETTUCE

STRAWBERRIES

and beets are helpful to each other. Lettuce is assisted by either carrots or strawberries grown nearby.

Nasturtiums, in addition to producing bright flowers, give sturdy assistance in repelling pests. They are known to discourage aphids and squash bugs, and thus are friendly neighbors to plants that would be attacked by these pests.

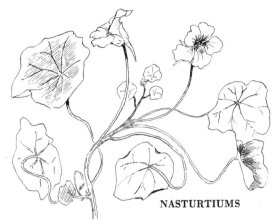

NASTURTIUMS

There are insects that are friendly to plants and trees, in that they attack other insects that are pests. Guardian ants that are non-herbivorous (ones that don't eat plants) are reported to live in trees and fight off the invasion of leaf-eating insects. Ants are said to protect orchids against the threat of caterpillars. And without insects, of course, many plants could not propagate, or reproduce, and would disappear.

In order to survive, many of our food plants, except the cereals, have depended for pollination on an alliance between flowers and insects. This includes both trees and plants that provide our fruits and vegetables. Some of the work is done by man, by artificial pollination, but in many plants it is the insect's job.

In pollination, both plants and insects benefit. The insects want the food found in the nectar (a sweet juice) and in the pollen (a fine, sticky dust) provided by the flower. And when they collect this from the flowers, they also distribute pollen from one flower to another. Some of the pollen clings to their furry or hairy bodies as they brush against it, to be brushed off again against another flower.

35

For fertilization, the germ tube of the pollen grain must reach the ovule of a flower. Usually this pollen must come from another flower. Some flowers are self-pollinated, with both pollen and ovule provided by the same flower. But in general, either the resulting fruit of self-pollination is poor, or such pollination is impossible. So the insects are responsible for much of the pollination.

The fact that bees pollinate flowers is well-known. But unless you have been watching a garden carefully, you may not have noticed that butterflies, moths, flies, wasps, and beetles also serve to pollinate flowers. The insects feed on the flowers' nectar, and in the course of doing so, transport pollen from flower to flower. And though the bees use pollen itself for food, as well as nectar, enough pollen clings to their hairy legs to pollinate the flowers they visit. The bees tend to visit the same kind of flower while it is in bloom, and this is part of the partnership pattern, for flowers must be pollinated by their own type of pollen.

One-sided relationships among plants are illustrated by

BEE ON THISTLE

the parasite plants. Parasites live on other plants or trees and are dependent upon them for nourishment. The word parasite originally meant "one frequenting the table of the rich or living at another's expense," according to Webster's Dictionary. Mistletoe is usually considered a parasite, taking all and giving nothing, sometimes even harming the tree to which it clings with its heavy overgrowth. But a theory has been advanced that mistletoe is part of a mutual-benefit arrangement, absorbing nourishment from the tree in the spring and summer and sending stored-up nourishment back to the tree in the winter.

A completely dependent partnership exists between the yucca plant and the yucca moth. The moth depends on the plant for seeds for its larvae to feed on, and the yucca depends on the moth for pollination in order to grow seeds. The moth

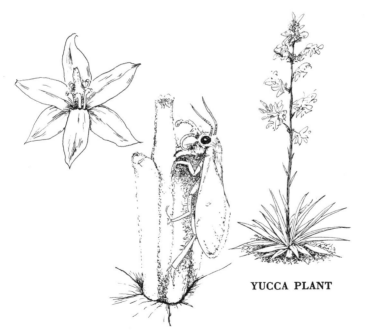

YUCCA PLANT

YUCCA MOTH GATHERING POLLEN

gathers pollen from one yucca flower and takes it on to another flower. In the second flower it lays its eggs. Now seeds can begin to grow in the yucca flower that is pollinated. And the moth eggs grow and hatch the larvae, which feed on the yucca seeds. All very convenient, and both partners are satisfied.

Fungi play a role in symbiosis. Lady's slippers are said to transplant more easily when a familiar root fungus is in the soil. Another such association, called mycorrhiza, occurs between a certain fungus and the roots of bog plants, some heaths, and certain trees such as birches.

An alliance that is really a necessity is found in lichens. Lichens are actually compound plants. They are formed by a combination of alga and fungus, which live off each other. The fungus takes up and holds water and mineral salts from the soil; by the action of sunlight on the chlorophyll of the alga, the water held by the fungus is combined with carbon dioxide from the air to form food for both plants, a process called *photosynthesis*. Since the chlorophyll of the green alga enables it to perform this transformation, it would therefore seem the more important partner.

RED-CRESTED CLADONIA

WALL LICHEN

PARMELIA

Partners, allies, companions—these terms come from man's own experience. But plants can vividly demonstrate the meaning of the words.

V

Seed Dispersal

MANY PLANTS show unusual methods of seed dispersal, or the scattering of their seeds. Some, for example, shoot out their seeds as far as fifty feet. They will do this of their own accord, but the action can be triggered with a touch. This form of dispersal permits new offspring of the plant to grow at distances which are sometimes considerable, thus aiding in ensuring the survival of the plant species.

Some familiar plants scatter seeds in this fashion. We can watch them and see the performance when it occurs naturally. Peas in the vegetable garden will throw out their seeds when the pods are dry enough. The pods twist, splitting open, and the seeds are scattered widely.

Flowering plants in the garden, such as violets and pansies, that we may not have noticed showering out their seeds, will repay close watching. As the petals drop, the tiny fruit of these plants can be seen. Gradually, the fruit will open to show the seeds lying in little saucers. The edges of these saucers draw in slowly, the layers drying and pressing together, squeezing the seeds until at last the seeds will be sprayed out.

The balsam family, *Balsaminaceae,* contributes well-

 BALSAM

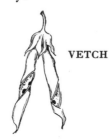 VETCH

 PANSY

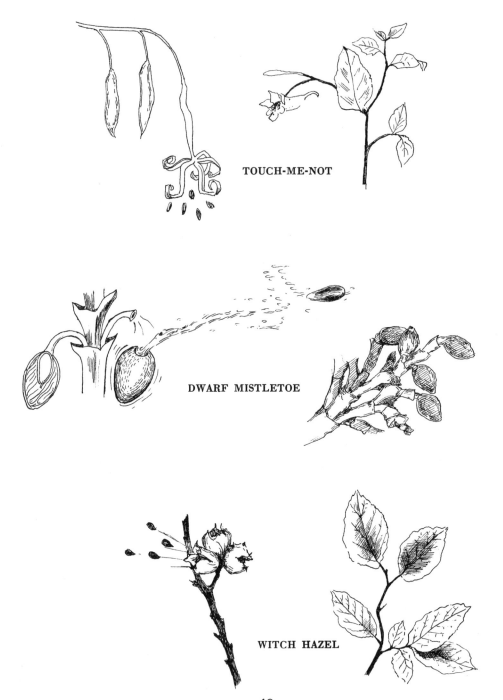

TOUCH-ME-NOT

DWARF MISTLETOE

WITCH HAZEL

known plants that shoot out their seeds. One genus—*Impatiens* —is known for plants which have seed pods described as explosive. These include garden and house plants, notably the common garden balsam. Garden balsam has fruit that separates into five segments that curl and break as they ripen. A touch will send the seed flying out.

Two lowly members of the *Impatiens* branch of the family, jewelweed and snapweed, found in gardens only by accident, shoot out their seeds also. Jewelweed is better known by the name touch-me-not. This name has developed because a touch triggers the seeds.

Dwarf mistletoe, a relative of the common mistletoe we know, also shoots out seeds with great force. It has been called the popgun plant. Its seeds have been observed to travel thirty to fifty feet. From the tree where the mistletoe clings they are sent to other trees where new parasite growths will form.

Wood sorrel, or *Oxalis montana,* has its fruit capsules which will split at a touch and deliver the seeds. It is noisy about this, and the sound of the seeds shooting out has been compared to the crack of a pistol shot.

Witch hazel also sends out its seeds with a sound effect. This can be observed in the fall, when the fruit ripens and the woody capsule containing the seeds dries and shrinks, finally discharging the seeds explosively.

Plants have many methods of scattering their seeds and sending them to new areas. Some, like the garden pea, have seed pods that twist. This twisting action not only opens the pod and discharges the seeds but, when the pods are dropped, often results in motion along the ground that moves the seeds away from the parent plant. One of the gesnerads, *Streptocarpus* (the

STREPTOCARPUS

name deriving from the Greek words for fruit and twisted), has fruit that is spirally twisted. As it dries, the spiral untwists, releasing the seeds.

Sweet-gum seeds are contained in balls suspended from twigs. When the balls dry and the wind blows them, the seeds are scattered.

Seeds of some plants are equipped to be airborne. You probably know the wings of the maple seeds and have seen milkweed seeds drifting through the air. Tufts of silk and silky fuzz permit many seeds to be carried by the wind. Seeds of the cottonwood tree have silky fuzz. Thistle seeds and cattail seeds are also airborne types. Dandelion seeds, and those of cotton and wild salsify, have parachutelike devices. Other seeds that travel by air include those of the goldenrod, clematis, and fireweed.

Some seeds have been termed "hitchhikers," since they

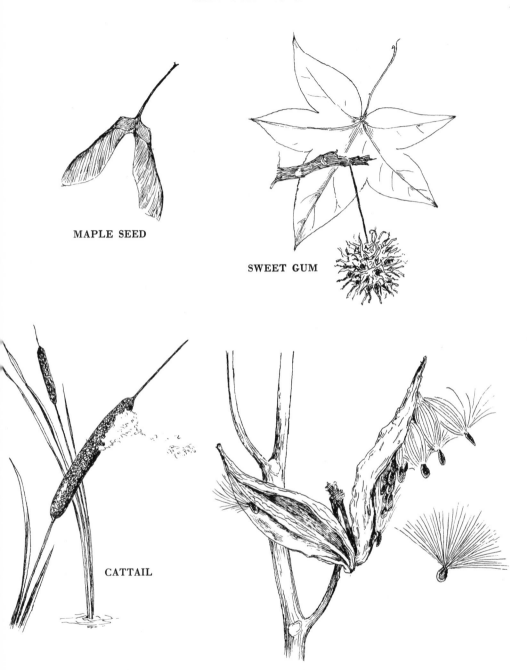

MAPLE SEED

SWEET GUM

CATTAIL

MILKWEED SEEDS COMING OUT OF PODS

43

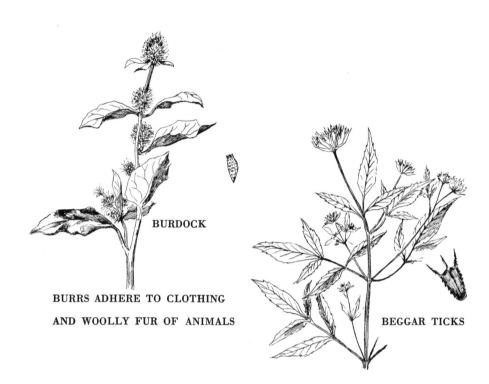

BURDOCK

BURRS ADHERE TO CLOTHING
AND WOOLLY FUR OF ANIMALS

BEGGAR TICKS

WIND WITCH

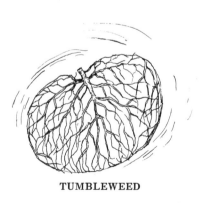

TUMBLEWEED

attach themselves to animals and humans who may brush against them. The burdock is an example that you may easily encounter. When you start picking off the burrlike fruit that has fastened itself to your clothes, note the tiny hooked prickles with which it holds on while being taken for its ride.

Other seeds that attach themselves to passersby are those of *Desmodium canadense*, better known under their common names of beggar's-lice and beggar-ticks. They catch on to animals as well as people, and will start growing wherever they are pulled off and thrown to the ground.

Some seeds can be carried across country by plants that roll. Tumbleweed dries and separates from its roots, blowing across the plains in a large, ball-shaped mass. The seeds are scattered great distances away in this manner.

A similar plant that grows in Russia is named the wind witch. Its branches gradually bend down against the ground, pressing there, so that the taproot, or central root, is forced up from the earth. Then the plant can roll with the wind, scattering seeds.

H. E. Gates, of Cornell University, in a paper called "Some Notes on Seed Dispersal," suggests another method of transportation. Some seeds are sticky, equipped with a mucilage type of substance. These can become attached to the feet of birds, and thus carried to new growing areas.

An herb, the common sage called salvia, has earned itself a special name—the ski-jump plant—because of its method of seed dispersal. As the wind moves the plant, the seeds slide down the calyx, or green base of the flower, along a tube pointed away from the plant. Then they scatter out at the end of the "ski run."

NEEDLE GRASS

Perhaps the most unusual performance is put on by the plants that place their own seeds in the ground. Long filaments, or threads, called awns, are fastened to one end of the seeds of some plants. Seeds of needle grass have awns, and so do those of animated oats. The awns are sensitive to changes in humidity, and will move, twisting the seeds about, when damp. A bend in the awns assists a spiral movement as dampness affects them. Moisture causes the awns to move, untwisting; tension builds, and when the seed pod breaks, the seeds are sent traveling out.

This movement of the awns can do double duty. Often the twisting motion will force the pointed front end of the seed ahead. When the position is right, the seed will be forced into the ground.

The peanut, too, can plant itself. A tendril of the plant bends down, pushing the peanut seed into the ground. The next time you eat a handful of peanuts, remember they are the seeds that are self-planted.

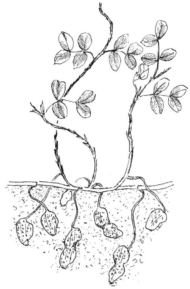

PEANUT

VI

Light-giving Plants

Bioluminescence is the giving off of light from living matter, caused by internal oxidation. When oxygen combines with other substances, energy is released—in the form of light or heat or both.

Certain flowers and plants give off faint, glowing light, which is caused by phosphorescent chemicals in the plant. There are water plants that glow, too, and are one cause of the ocean's phosphorescence at certain places. And luminous mosses are found in some European caves that glow with a jeweled effect.

On an otherwise dark night in Burma, during World War II, a soldier wrote a letter home to his wife by the greenish glow of a cluster of luminous mushrooms, called Mycena.

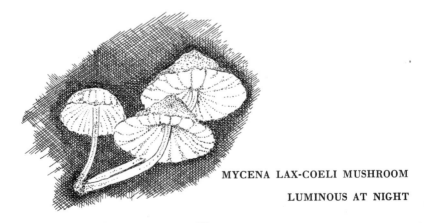

MYCENA LAX-COELI MUSHROOM

LUMINOUS AT NIGHT

But plants that give off light may be seen in your own home garden. Some such plants are the nasturtium, the common and African marigold (one record mentioning double flowers of the common marigold), the Oriental and hairy poppy, the sunflower, and the scarlet verbena. Sometimes flashes of light have been observed from flower to flower; at other times, a general phosphorescent effect is seen.

To discover your flowers giving off light needs somewhat the patience of stalking wild game. It also requires careful attention to atmospheric conditions. Early reports of bioluminescence in flowers deal more with the surprising effect than with the details of how it might be seen again.

An early authenticated report of the luminosity of flowering plants traces back to the eighteenth century and to Linnaeus, whose floral clock has already been mentioned. It was he who worked out the first system for naming plants, the basis of what is used today.

In the summer of 1762, his daughter, Christina Linné, walking in the garden, observed nasturtium flowers giving off flashes of light. Then Linnaeus himself, together with other scientists, witnessed this on several evenings.

Since that time, observers have seen flashes of light given out by nasturtium leaves as well as flowers. A report was given by a Canon Russel, who noted luminous nasturtium leaves. He placed a leaf under a microscope in a dark room and found that the leaf was visible by its own light.

The canon also recorded light shown by marigolds, and made sure of other witnesses. Here conditions are mentioned. The time was evening, from dusk toward dark, and the weather was sultry.

Goethe, the famous German poet and dramatist, while accompanied by a friend who also observed it, reported seeing flashes of light from the flowers of the Oriental poppy.

Other flowers have been observed to show luminosity. In the *Gardener's Chronicle,* in 1859, a report is given of flashes of light passing from one scarlet verbena plant to another. In this record, the phenomenon was seen repeatedly about sunset, when the day had been hot and the ground was dry. Luminosity was noted especially when conditions were dry but a thunderstorm was approaching. The point was made that the air was then charged with electricity.

In commenting on light-giving plants, in the early quarter of this century, E. Fitch Daglish, whose book on plant life is listed in the bibliography, describes a vine found in South America named the Cipo. "The Cipo," he wrote, "exudes a luminous sap in considerable quantities, giving rise to a rain of flaming drops, which cover the leaves and branches of the vegetation on which they fall, as with a veil of living fire."

The fact that light sometimes shines from decaying wood was noted as early as the fourth century B.C. by the Greek philosopher and naturalist Aristotle. This light comes from the threads of fungi in the wood. As was mentioned in Chapter IV, the fungus of lichen uses the alga for photosynthesis. The product of photosynthesis—carbohydrates—in the living branch or tree, is used for food by the fungus in the decaying wood.

Luminescent fungi need the oxygen in air to give off light. Experiments have proved that without oxygen the fungus stops shining. Similarly, water plants get oxygen from the water. Oxidation, then, is necessary for luminescence. The combining of certain other substances with oxygen causes a release of energy—and the energy is released as light. The luminous fungi may be seen more easily by night, but they go right on sending out light in the daytime.

Mushrooms are a kind of fungus. Fungi do not have roots and leaves; instead, they are composed of a mass of tiny threads. This mass of threads is called the mycelium. It grows at great speed, and you have probably been surprised by mushrooms that seemed to pop up on the lawn overnight. The mushroom cap you see is the fruit, holding the spores, and underground is the mycelium that sends up the mushroom caps. At night you may see luminous mushrooms, or toadstools. Experiments with luminous mushrooms showed that they went on shining when covered with water but stopped when covered by boiling water, from which most of the oxygen had evaporated.

In the ocean, an important part of nourishment for sea dwellers is plankton—drifting masses of living "soup"—that is composed of tiny forms of plant and animal life. Among these are floating plants of algae. And there are tiny drifting marine organisms that function as plants, some of which have animal characteristics—the dinoflagellates. Masses of these dinoflagellates can be seen glowing in darkness.

If you wish to watch for a light-giving effect among the more familiar garden flowers, the best time would be on a summer evening near dusk. And the best weather conditions, according to reported recordings of such sightings, would exist at the end of a dry hot day when a thunderstorm was gathering.

If you see this light-giving effect, call other witnesses to substantiate your report and perhaps to add observed details. Note the type of plant or flower, the exact light effect, the time, and the weather. If you have a camera that can take pictures in dusky or fading light, it would be useful to record your observations.

PLANT	LUMINESCENCE
Plants Whose Bioluminescence Is Well-known	
Luminous mosses (e.g., *Schistostega osmundacea*) in caves of Europe	jeweled light on walls of caves
Plants Whose Bioluminescence Is Less Well-known	
Nasturtiums (first observed by Linnaeus' daughter in 1762)	flashes of light: most often from flowers, occasionally from leaves
Marigolds (common and African; double blossoms of common)	rapid vibrations of light: sometimes flashes, flower to flower, petal to petal; sometimes phosphorescent effect
Oriental poppies (first seen by Goethe in 1799)	flashes of light from flowers
Scarlet verbena (first seen by several witnesses in 1859)	repeated flashes from plant to plant

VII

Electroculture

WOULD YOU LIKE to have flowers in your garden that tower above those of your neighbors, with a lavish spread of bloom? Would you like to grow tomatoes that measure a foot around? These are some of the dramatic claims of the proponents of *electroculture,* the stimulation of plant growth by treatment with electricity.

The successful use of electricity to improve plant growth has been established in the laboratory. Now it is spreading to backyard flowerbeds and vegetable gardens. Home gardeners can aim at the record of the University of Massachusetts, which has reported raising radish plants that produced a 50 percent heavier yield by the use of electricity.

Various methods are used in electroculture. The one most easily used by home gardeners is that by which atmospheric electricity is attracted to the plant and to the area surrounding it. When this happens, an electrical field (i.e., a charged atmosphere) is set up, which stimulates the activity, and thus the growth, of the plant cells.

Metal is an excellent conductor of electricity; we use steel lightning rods to attract atmospheric electricity and conduct it quickly and safely into the ground. Metal, in the form of wires or tin cans, can also be used to attract electricity to flower gardens or vegetable beds.

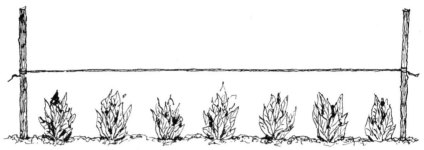

A COPPER WIRE STRETCHED OVER A ROW OF PLANTS
IS A SIMPLE METHOD OF ELECTROCULTURE

Copper wire, strung from metal posts set at the ends of rows of plants, is one method of electroculture. The wire should stretch closely above the plants but never touch them. As the plants grow, the wire above each row of plants should be lifted higher.

Another method is to use a circle of copper wire around each plant. A stake is driven into the ground beside the plant. The wire is fastened to the stake, leading out in a wide circle that encloses the plant but does not touch it.

A third method is to use coffee cans, or other large tin cans, with the tops and bottoms removed. There are two versions of this method. In one, a plant is set inside each tin can. Favorable results have also been reported from placing tin cans *beside* a row of seedlings. The cans should be sunk about two inches into the soil, in a row beside the seedlings.

Tomatoes grown by a combination of two of these methods, each plant in a coffee can and all of them under a copper wire, were reported to have grown fourteen-foot plants. Other reports of home use of electroculture include the production of peas in continual bloom, with three pickings from the same vines; a grapevine that grew twenty feet from seed in a year, and radishes that grew large enough to eat in four days.

Flowers also showed effective results. Chrysanthemum plants had unusually strong growth and produced lavish flowers. A canna plant reached seven feet in height, against the average five-foot height of plants not treated with electricity. Gardenias and magnolias showed good results, while roses reached a height of eight feet, against the four feet previously shown, and produced very lavish blooms.

All of these reports and others have been made by happy gardeners who were satisfied with the solid results of electroculture. What is needed now is the keeping of precise records of such experiments. Not only would this help others who want to try electroculture at home and would profit from the experience of others, but also, an important contribution would be made by reports which conformed to scientific standards. This is necessary if the results of the experiments are to be accepted by scientists.

When is a report a correct report? It is a record of specific data kept regularly, as to such things as height and strength and speed of growth of plants. It gives a description of the method of electroculture used. It also includes a careful report on control plants, which are plants that are grown under identical conditions to the plants being tested, with the exception of the feature that is being tested. The comparison of the experimental plants with the control plants, at intervals, would be important. And there should be photographs of the plants, taken at different stages of growth. Such a record would be worth the time taken, in order to have acceptable scientific proof of the results.

The basis for keeping an accurate record is shown at the end of this chapter.

You may want to start by growing unusually large vegetables and tall flowering plants with luxuriant bloom, and let the records go until a second season. But if you have dramatic success, you may wish you had kept a proper record so that your results could receive scientific recognition.

General interest in electroculture is fairly recent. But scientific experiments with it began as long ago as 1746, when the beneficial effect of electricity on the growth of myrtle trees was first reported. This was followed by research in France by Abbé Nolet, who announced that he had gotten favorable results from his experiments in the use of electricity to speed up seed germination.

Research continued in different countries for a century and a half before receiving much general attention. In the first decade of this century, successful results were obtained in the United States at the Hatch Experiment Station of Massachusetts Agricultural College.

Different methods of applying electricity to a small number of plants had shown that it had a decided effect in promoting growth. But these early methods of electroculture were difficult to use over thousands of acres of field crops. To solve this problem, Dr. Fry decided to try to apply an electric current to the seeds of the plants.

The method was simple, but needed to be carried out with care. The grain was steeped in salt water, a good conductor of electricity. The salt solution and seed were placed in a tank, and a current of electricity was passed through the water by means of electrodes attached to opposite walls of the tank. Then the seed was taken out and dried.

The results of this work, reported by Charles A. Mercier, were called "a revolution in agriculture." Mercier continued Fry's work, and English farmers who tried the process became enthusiasts. Not only was their crop yield larger, but the plants were stronger and more resistant to adverse weather. An observer for the United States Government advised wide trials of the method in this country.

Research on different techniques of seed germination have been carried on in this country, with notable results in 1962 with corn and apple seeds that were treated with 220 volts of electricity while embedded in moist sand.

The effects of electricity in promoting growth of plants has been worked out with precision. This work has been published by the University of Massachusetts (formerly the Massachusetts Agricultural College, mentioned earlier). Two research projects undertaken by the university showed interesting results; the first recorded the growth of a tomato plant whose size was increased by electricity, and the second showed the result of an experiment with radish plants in an electrically charged case; the average gain in weight of the electrically stimulated plants over the control plants was over 50 percent.

Drs. O. A. Brown, R. B. Stone, Jr., and Henry Andrews, in a report made in the magazine *Agricultural Engineering,* in 1957, comment on various methods of electrifying seeds:

"There are many ways to apply electric energy to living organisms. The simplest is to make the organism a part of an electric circuit and pass the current directly through it."

Further developments in the use of electricity to promote plant growth are foreseeable in the future. One such development may be the application of *piezoelectricity,* which is the name given electricity produced by squeezing or bending certain substances, such as the small crystals of bones. Two Japanese scientists, E. Fukada and I. Yusada, the former a physicist and the latter a bone surgeon, found that squeezing or bending a piece of bone produced these currents. In further research with a substance called collagen, which makes up part of the tissue of bones, these scientists tested collagen fibers, which are parallel to each other. They found that squeezing them at an angle produced strong electric currents, though squeezing them straight against sides of the fibers produced very little current.

The next step may be to apply this method to the cellular fibers of plants, so that a shift of position will set electric current flowing. The results of such stimulation remain to be seen.

While scientists carry on research projects that show the effects of electricity on plants and seeds, experiments also continue in home gardens. All that is needed is a patch of ground for a bed, the simple materials of wires and cans and stakes, and seeds or seedlings.

Experiments can be done in the garden with a variety of flowering plants and vegetables that have not been tested yet. And when the tall plants, the lavish flowers and large vegetables result in successful experiments, if a record has been kept according to the method suggested below, the experiments can take their place as research, as well as fun. It's nice to be able to have your tomato in a permanent record and eat it too.

Scientific Experiments

*How to set up experiments with plants
and record them scientifically*

If one wishes to set up an experiment to demonstrate the effects of electricity, or any other factor, on plants, which will be meaningful, the rules below should be followed:

1. Start with seeds or plants as uniform as possible.
2. Have a set of untreated, or control, plants.
3. Use an adequate number of plants properly duplicated.
4. Keep all other factors constant except for the one being studied.
5. Record the results in a constant manner.
6. Repeat the experiment.

In order to start with uniform seeds or plants it may be necessary to discard the unusually small or large plants from the available supply. Obviously the sets of controls and treated plants should be as alike as possible.

Any experiment without controls is worthless as far as creditable evidence goes. In a simple type of experiment one should have at least as many control plants as treated ones. In more complex experiments where the factor being tested is used at different strengths, or concentrations, etc., one set of controls equal in number to those at one concentration is usually adequate. It is not possible to generalize as to the number of seeds or plants. Seeds are commonly tested in lots of a hundred. The number of plants probably should be at least half a dozen, perhaps several dozen. One of the main reasons for adequate numbers is the idea of replication or repetitions. This is to get around the inevitable variation in plants. A significant result from the factor being studied must be greater in magnitude than the normal variation between plants. In other words the greater the variability within the controls or within the treated plants, the more difficult it is to demonstrate a real difference between control and treated plants.

It should be apparent that all factors except the one being tested must be held constant. This applies also to the conditions before the experiment actually starts. Factors to watch for are seeds or plants from the same source and variety, and uniform temperature, light, soil, fertilizing and watering.

Results or records may be taken in many ways depending on circumstances and the effect one is trying to demonstrate. Sometimes several different kinds of results can be taken, for example, the earliness of blooming and the weight of the fruit. The records must be kept separate for the different lots of replicates or subgroups tested; e.g., measure each replicate plant or lots of seeds separately. Only in this way can we have a record of normal variation. In a sophisticated experiment a statistical analysis of the results will be made by appropriate and recognized mathematical procedures and formulae. The purpose of this is to demonstrate objectively that the difference between the treated and controls is significantly greater than that within the plants of the controls or treated sets. That is, that the difference is a real one and probably not just the variation that could happen by chance. Photographs can be a very useful and convincing supplement to numerical records. However, the pictures should be of typical results and not limited to the very best of the treated plants.

Finally, the whole experiment should be repeated at another time, e.g., the next week or month or year. It is much better to repeat an experiment using adequate numbers of plants than it is to run only one large experiment. If you cannot repeat your own results, how can you expect anyone else to verify them?

VIII

Response to Sound

THERE HAS BEEN much discussion about whether or not plants respond to sound. Some people maintain that plants grow better when they are talked to, sung to, or when music is played nearby. Others think this is nonsense.

Two scientists working in India, T. C. N. Singh and S. Ponniah, have reported successful results of music on plant growth.

Dr. Richard Klein, formerly at the New York Botanical Gardens and now professor of botany at the University of Vermont, gave a lighthearted but scientifically precise report on his own findings in 1965. For a period of regulated testing, plants were subjected to an unusual program of recorded music, ranging from Gregorian chants of the Benedictine Monks of En Calcat to "I Want to Hold Your Hand," sung by the Beatles, and "The Stripper," played by David Rose and orchestra. The summary of results states: "There was no significant effect of any of the musical selections on the growth of vegetative or reproductive structures of the test plants. Variations in growth pattern could not be observed; there was no leaf abscission traceable to the influence of 'The Stripper' nor could we observe any stem mutation in plants exposed to the Beatles." Dr. Klein notes in the discussion of the experiments that the results do not completely answer the question of a possible effect of sound on the growth of plants.

One thing that has been definitely established in this field is the response of plants to ultrasound. Ultrasonic vibrations are sounds beyond the limit of human hearing. Bats, dolphins and dogs are among the creatures that can hear sounds in the ultrasonic range. And now it has been proved that plants react to ultrasound, although we can't say that they "hear" it.

Dr. Hubert J. Dyer of Brown University, together with Dr. W. L. Nyborg, in a scientific paper presented at the Third International Conference on Medical Electronics in London, in 1960, reported on characteristics of intercellular motion induced by ultrasound. The experiments showed movement of various kinds set up in plant cells by ultrasonic excitation of cell walls. This excitation was done by bringing a vibrating needle tip into contact or near contact with a small portion of cell wall.

Among other results, an aggregation of intracellular bodies in a small region over the vibrating portion of the membrane was observed, and also particle displacements which persisted when the sound was on and relaxed when it was off.

Studies in this field, according to these scientists in another paper, have interest because of the possibilities "that further study will provide additional knowledge about the effect of ultrasound on biological cells, and that a useful tool for nonsurgical manipulation of cellular contents will result."

In a compilation of the abstracts of the 1966 meetings of the Federation of American Societies for Experimental Biology, definite results of the effect of ultrasound on plants were reported. These included earliness of germination, an increase in root length in a given time after treatment, as compared to control plants, and increase in plant weight.

To return to the question of plants' response to music, and the controversy about this, and moving outside the laboratory, the field is open for amateur experiment. Interested persons can observe a selection of plants with music played nearby regularly over a period of time, and compare the results with a control group of similar plants growing without music.

IX

Atomic Gardens and Farms

ATOMIC GARDENS and farms are no longer found only in the worlds of space fiction, but now can be grown on our own planet. You can even experiment in your own garden with plants and seeds that have been irradiated, and thus have a good chance of providing mutations—plants with entirely new characteristics and appearances. These are the most modern of plant performers.

On the atomic farms of scientific laboratories, research is being done to improve plants. For example, scientists are concerned with producing changes in plants that will make them more resistant to disease or will produce a higher yield in crops. These changes can now be made by mutation through radiation much more quickly than was ever possible before.

A mutation is a definite change in the genes which regulate the form, nature or qualities of a plant or animal, and this change is one that can be inherited. Mutations occur, of course, in nature, and if the change is one that helps the plant or animal to survive better than before, new plants produced by the mutated one (or the offspring of mutated organisms) will also be able to survive better, and so, gradually, replace all of the original forms of these living things. Men learned many centuries ago to take advantage of and to speed up this process of change by selective breeding of plants and animals. Such a

65

process, however, is still slow, for desired changes may take many generations before they become established, or widely useful. Now, however, the process can be speeded up by irradiating plants with cobalt 60 or other sources of ionizing radiation.

Cobalt 60 is a radioactive form or isotope of cobalt, a metallic element. It gives off gamma rays, one of the three kinds of ray emitted by radioactive substances. (Any radioactive substance is highly dangerous, of course, and must be handled with extreme caution.) These rays, like X rays, penetrate many substances readily. But they are stopped with fair effectiveness by some heavy elements such as lead.

On an experimental farm at Brookhaven National Laboratories on Long Island, a large amount of cobalt 60 is contained in a steel pipe that can be lowered into a two-ton lead cylinder and then raised again as desired, the raising and lowering being controlled at a distance. The radioactive cobalt is shielded by the lead when it is in the cylinder. Plants are placed in concentric circles, with the cobalt cylinder in the center. When desired, the cobalt is raised out of its lead shield in order to expose the plants to radiation.

Both government-sponsored and private experiments are being carried out at farms around the country, in laboratories such as the one at Oak Ridge, Tennessee, and at research centers and college experimental stations. The Atomic Energy Commission and state agricultural stations cooperate in this work. Sometimes seeds, plants and young trees are sent to the laboratory at Brookhaven, to be exposed to radiation, and then the succeeding tests during growth are made locally by the persons or groups concerned. In this way, grains and fruits of an improved sort have been developed in different parts of the country.

Experiments with flowers that have received gamma radiation from radioactive cobalt also show interesting results. Many flowers may be distorted as a result of radiation, and be interesting only as scientific curiosities. But others may be newly attractive, or have valuable characteristics such as superior strength or resistance to disease.

A satisfactory mutant—a new flowering plant with inheritable characteristics varying from those of the parent plants —took more time to develop in previous times, as did improved types of field crops. Flowers with varying petals, new colors, or different sizes, were eventually developed, but it took a long time before a good result was obtained.

Now, with the use of atomic radiation, many more mutations are produced than would occur in nature. More mutations mean a wider range of new types to choose from, in a shorter time. There is a much greater chance of gaining desirable flowering plants quickly.

These improved plants are here to stay, because radiation changes the genes of the plants which carry hereditary traits. So a double flower of a kind that didn't exist before, a dwarfed plant, a flower with newly shaped petals, passes on its new qualities to following generations of plants.

Plants and seeds that have been exposed to atomic radiation are not radioactive themselves, and are entirely safe. They can be handled, and their fruit and seeds eaten, without any danger.

Natural mutations—plants that have entirely new characteristics and appearances—occur constantly and very slowly over centuries of time; as with animals that have evolved throughout history, a change in structure may occur once in a great while, and the change may or may not enable the plant or animal to survive better in its environment. If the mutation is a helpful one, the plant generally survives and outlives its less sturdy ancestors. The same results, of course, can now be achieved in a relatively short period of time by radiation of seeds or plants with cobalt 60.

X

Cold and Plant Life

THE EFFECT OF COLD on plants and on seeds has been noted and made use of for some time. Buds of woody trees and shrubs of the temperate zone must withstand severe winter cold. After a mild winter, they may fail to bloom. Other buds which may bloom prematurely during a warm, early spring are later killed by frost. Some seeds will produce only dwarf plants unless they are subjected to nearly freezing temperatures before planting.

Preserving flowers in their natural state by freezing, for purposes of research, has been developed more recently. And the preservation of pollen and seeds by deep freezing is also a recent development.

The influence of low temperatures on flowering is called *vernalization*. This name was first used in Russia, the word meaning to make springlike; our word is a translation of the Russian word *yaravoe*, from *yara*, or spring.

More than one hundred years ago it was known that early flowering of certain plants could be speeded up by low-temperature treatment. This treatment was applied in this century with the vernalization of winter grains. More modern research covers a wider variety of crops. Precise reports, for example, show the effect of cold on peas and tomatoes in hastening budding.

The vernalization of seeds was studied before that of the entire plant. The result with grains has special importance for

India and other countries where conditions of drought or flood prevail. A few days' difference in the maturing of a crop may mean the success or failure of the harvest and survival or famine for large masses of people.

Vernalization of the entire plant, instead of the seed, was worked out successfully with some plants, such as celery. And study is now going on with plants that can respond to vernalization of both types—the seed and the whole plant.

Timing of the application of cold varies with different plants, as does the degree of cold and the length of period of application.

Cold is used to preserve flowers in a dramatically natural state for long periods of time. Flowers have been kept in good condition at low temperatures, at Columbia University, for over five years.

At the New York Botanical Garden, flowers wait in their plastic envelopes at subzero temperatures. Lilies, irises, tropical flowers such as some of the gesnerads—they have a fairy-tale aspect, like Sleeping Beauty flowers, lying in the freezer drawers and looking as if they had just been picked. When these chilled flowers are needed, they are taken out of the cold and used for classwork, for sketching, and for dissection.

Cold is used for many purposes in botany. Its effect on yeasts and fungi is being studied, for possible long-term storage of these plants on space flights. Low-temperature storage has its values on earth, too. Unusual types of fungi and yeasts, of service to medicine or industry, can be stored till needed.

Cryogenics, the application and effects of very low temperatures, also has a place in plant storage and propagation. Liquid nitrogen, one of the liquids used in cryogenics, is used to store pollen. Preservation of pollen is important, for example, in crossing two varieties of pine trees. The Northern pine produces good wood but grows slowly, and the Southern pine produces poorer wood but grows more rapidly. The two kinds of tree germinate at different times of year, making cross-pollination impossible—except through cryogenics. Pollen of one type of tree, stored in the liquid nitrogen, can be used for cross-pollination later with that of the second type of tree.

Long-range storage is being studied at the Boyce Thompson Institute for Plant Research. There, seeds of garden plants, such as tomato and onion seeds, are being kept in deep freeze. This research is concerned with the length of time the seeds will stay alive. Some of these experiments may last over one hundred years.

We can't try experiments in cryogenics at home, and we don't want to wait a century for results. But we can freeze flowers. Though flowers keep better at temperatures near zero, an experiment in the refrigerator or freezer is worth trying. Place your flower in a plastic bag and seal it tightly—one way is by dipping the edges of the bag in melted paraffin. Then set the bag in a box so the flower won't get bruised, in the freezer or at the back of the freezing compartment of your refrigerator. Experiment to find out how long you can keep a flower in good condition, so it looks freshly picked. It won't stay in shape for a long time after you remove it from the freezer, so a sketch or photograph should be made of it at once if you want to keep a record of its appearance.

XI

Healing Plants and Plant Hunters

WHILE SOME PLANTS perform with spectacular visual effects, others perform with curative effects. Long ago, most medicines were gained from plants. With no laboratories and modern scientific methods to depend upon, it was important to know which plant produced repeated cures for a specific ailment. And old records give accounts of such plant lore.

Of course, there was a certain amount of superstition mixed in with those early cures, and more than a touch of witchcraft. Some early remedies, for example, were wild rose and garlic, to be used as a protection against vampires and werewolves; the herb dock was recommended to break a fairy spell; and another herb, wormwood, was believed to be a remedy for the bite of a sea serpent.

WORMWOOD

Out of the early mixture of facts and fancies about cures from plants, or plant drugs, however, came some solid, proven cures. As Dr. Louis Lasagna pointed out in *The Doctors' Dilemmas,* while many ancient folk remedies originated in ignorance and superstition, it would be wrong to assume that all such remedies lack some basic beneficial effect. Quinine and ephedrine, he said, were used in crude preparations long before modern chemists were able to isolate them in pure form. Digitalis, one of the most widely prescribed medical remedies, was discovered by the 18th-century physician-botanist Withering. Dr. Withering analyzed a mixture of herbs that his country patients used for the treatment of a variety of ills, including chest pains and dropsy. The essential drug, he found, came from the foxglove plant—and thus was made one of the major advances in the treatment of heart failure.

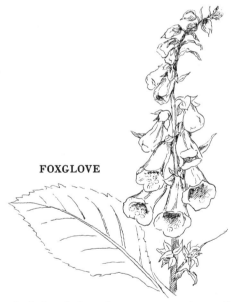

FOXGLOVE

We are indebted for the preservation of herbal remedies and knowledge of curative plants through the Dark Ages to the monks who cultivated their gardens and kept their records of healing plants. The monks also can be credited with the Latin and Greek basis for so many botanical names.

Helpful curative plants have been found not only in the old-time remedies of England and Europe and America, but also in the present-day use of them among primitive tribes. Indian snakeroot is one such plant. For centuries, this plant was legendary in Africa and in the more primitive parts of India, as a provider of strength, as a cure for snakebite poisoning, and as an aid in mental illness. More enlightened observation indicated that the plant did indeed have curative power, especially in the treatment of high blood pressure.

This plant is listed as *rauvolfia* by Linnaeus, but the present term is *rauwolfia*. The most important of the plant's components was found to be reserpine. And among the varieties

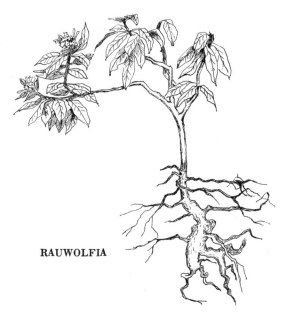

RAUWOLFIA

of the plant now used as drug sources is *Rauwolfia serpentina*. The plant now is a valuable source of a drug used for lowering blood pressure. It is also the basis of many widely used tranquilizing drugs.

Curare, which gained a place in mystery stories as the native substance that was put on the tips of poison arrows, now has a medicinal position of importance. The plant from which this material was prepared was well-known to the jungle tribes of South America; it was studied in 1850 by Claude Bernard, the great physiologist, although its importance in medicine was not then known. Gradually, species of plants from which curare was made were gathered, and the resultant material was analyzed and tested. Today curare is used to relax muscles during surgery and during shock treatment, and as a treatment for spastic disorders.

With the growing realization that important cures might be found among the plants used as native remedies in remote parts of the world came the work of the plant hunters. Expeditions were launched to try to discover, among difficult and often dangerous conditions, plants which could be brought back to our laboratories for eventual sources of new drugs.

Reports that members of a faraway tribe used unknown plants for cures which had not yet been discovered set the plant hunters out to track down the botanicals.

Some of the values of these trips are explained by Nicole Maxwell, an explorer who has made repeated expeditions for plants in South American jungles, one of them among the headhunters of the Amazon (see bibliography). She has maintained contact with witch doctors in the deep jungle, and sometimes gained their confidence so they have shared with her their herbal knowledge—which they consider magic and are usually most reluctant to discuss.

"There is, of course, the reward of finally finding the plants you are searching for, after the early disappointments of a trip," Mrs. Maxwell observed. "There is always the hope that plants you bring back will be the basis for new drugs that will help attack disease. There's the excitement of tracking down rumors of cures that you don't believe at first, and then searching out a jungle tribe and finding a plant which seems to perform a new function in medicine. Research work on these plants for medicinal purposes, called pharmacognosy, is a rapidly growing field. And further, I have gained a respect for the knowledge and ability of many natives who might be dismissed by sophisticated medical practitioners as ignorant witch doctors. These natives know some of the things that our researchers have proved can outstrip our own information. And it is great fun to link up these remote workers with the white-coated medicine men in the city."

Aside from exotic plants, there are many ordinary and well-known plants that contribute to health and to disease cure and prevention. Spinach used to be valued chiefly as a source of iron; now it is known to be one of the plants rich in vitamin K, which helps blood coagulation. Cabbage is still served as a hot vegetable, but it is reported by doctors that the juice of raw cabbage benefits peptic ulcers and digestive complaints. Yams are usually thought of in connection with maple syrup and nutmeg for dinner, but the Mexican yams, now being grown in this country, are an important source of steroids, certain organic compounds, some of which have been used in the treatment of cancer.

Moldy bread doesn't seem a hopeful treatment for infection; but the molds on old bread were found to be beneficial, centuries before their more sophisticated appearance in antibiotics. Yeast is readily thought of in connection with baking; yeast plants also supply low-cost vitamins and protein. Algae are green plants to be scooped out of ponds and seawater; they are also a source of iodine, trace minerals, and nutritives.

So it goes with plants from near and far that help keep us in health and cure disease. They may be brought from a distant mountain or rain forest, or grow at our doorstep. We may have to find them, analyze them, and perfect drugs from them—but they are waiting to perform for our good health.

XII

Plants of the Future

GARDENS ON MARS may be in the future, but Mars gardens of another kind exist right now. These are the gardens grown by scientists, under the conditions believed to exist on Mars. These gardens have shown that the climate of Mars does not exclude the possibility of plant life. Martian environmental conditions —such as soil, water, atmosphere, and temperature—have been duplicated in laboratories as closely as possible, and certain fungi have been found to live under these conditions.

One of the leading scientists in this field, Dr. S. M. Siegel, has carried on many experiments, including those of a four-year contract with the National Aeronautics and Space Administration. Among Dr. Siegel's conclusions are those in a paper entitled "Martian Biology: the Experimentalist's Approach" of which he was the senior author: "Our results show that complex terrestrial organisms can survive and grow under conditions which constitute an extreme departure in one or more respects from the normal terrestrial environment. Of particular importance was the finding that tolerance of plants to low temperatures could be conditioned in a favorable manner by synthetic atmospheres low in oxygen."

Experiments which led to these conclusions showed that some of the higher plants, as well as fungi, could survive at low oxygen pressures. The planting material used—a mixture of soil and Perl-lome (a commercial derivative of perlite, a volcanic mineral)—corresponded to the volcanic material believed to be present on Mars's surface. Experiments also indicated that seeds could germinate without liquid water.

In the regular reports of the work carried on by Dr. Siegel and his associates under the NASA contract, many possibilities for extraterrestrial plant life are noted. The subject of extraterrestrial plant life—plants growing beyond the limits of the earth—is considered in general, with a special emphasis on Mars. It was found, for example, that the presence of gases considered lethal to life on earth did not eliminate multicellular life altogether. Salt tolerance and metal tolerance were studied, and the ability to extract and use a very small quantity of water satisfactorily.

Further studies as to possibilities of plant growth on Mars indicated the suitability of lichens to Martian conditions. This tolerance of lichens to environmental factors of Mars included resistance to ultraviolet radiation.

Studies of plants grown under Martian conditions, of Mars jars where these conditions are maintained, and of the so-called Mars gardens give us the chance to look into the future. It is possible to see which plants can be expected to adapt to life on Mars before a spaceship arrives there to collect a specimen. And more will be learned as the research continues.

Another promising area for future research is further knowledge about substances that affect plant growth. Some of these, developed by the plants themselves, have been studied, and research has progressed in their control. Other growth-control substances are man-made.

Growth substances in plants are sometimes called plant hormones. Experiments in Holland over half a century ago showed that a growth factor was present in the tip of a seedling; when it was removed from the tip it would stimulate the growth of a section of another plant to which it was applied. Cells in that area grew faster than in sections without the substance.

Eventually, chemical mixtures were developed which had the effect of auxin, one of the plant's growth substances, when applied to plants. Synthetic materials were also found that would retard growth as well as advance it.

In Japan, scientists discovered a growth regulator produced by a fungus. The fungus was called *Gibberella fujikuroi,* and the substance was named gibberellic acid, often called GA or gibberellin for short. Research is now going on in this country studying extended uses of gibberellin. Also there is much to be learned about its precise control so that the results of increased growth will be uniformly desirable.

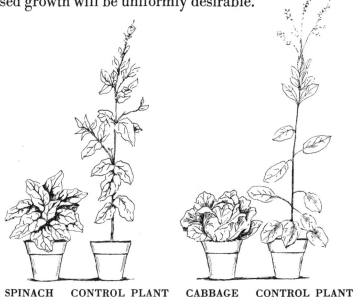

SPINACH   CONTROL PLANT   CABBAGE   CONTROL PLANT

In the meantime, special uses are being found for gibberellin; it is used by celery growers to gain longer petiole stalks, and in Australia to stimulate the growth of forage grass for winter grazing. Interesting results are also being obtained with flowers. Chemical substances that advance or retard growth of plants are on sale at garden centers and supply houses. Suggestions for their use are found in Chapter II.

A controversial point among scientists is the relationship between auxin and ethylene gas, a ripening agent. The effect of ethylene gas on citrus fruit was originally discovered accidentally, when fruit in a room heated by an electric stove, instead of the previously used kerosene stove, stayed green instead of ripening. Investigation showed that kerosene heating in an oxygen-poor room gave off a gas which caused the ripening. The gas was isolated as ethylene by U.S. Department of Agriculture scientists, and citrus growers then converted to airtight rooms where the proper concentration of ethylene to cause rapid and uniform ripening could be controlled.

Next, research workers at the University of California found that ethylene speeded up the ripening of avocados, and also resulted in the production of more ethylene by the plants. It was found that pears produced a small quantity of ethylene, and as a result paper wrappers are left on unripe pears, which tend to hold in the ethylene, and thus assist in ripening.

Scientists studying the effects of ethylene on young tomato plants found that the gas would cause the branches to bend sharply downward, a phenomenon called epinasty. Epinasty had already been noted as a result of treating a plant with auxins. Since epinasty involves the differential elongation of cells on the upper part of the branch, it began to look as if ethylene might be a cell-elongation factor similar to auxin.

The controversial positions, while research continues, fall into three main categories. One group of scientists takes the view that all or most of the effects of auxin would seem to be due to ethylene production which resulted from application of auxin. Thus, auxin would be a trigger for ethylene which, in turn, is the actual growth stimulant. Another group takes the position that although there is a close relation between auxin and ethylene, a causal relationship has not been established. The third group holds that ethylene is one of the complex of growth factors which act on plant cells.

The necessity of light for plants has been known for centuries. But the detailed information on the effect of light on plants is still being studied.

The three basic factors of light in its relation to plant growth are quality, the color composition of the light; quantity, the light's intensity; and duration, the amount of time that the plant receives light in a twenty-four-hour period.

Light is needed by the plant for the energy gained from it, which can be transferred to the plant cells. It is needed for photosynthesis. Without red and blue light, efficient photosynthesis would not be possible, and the plants would lack nourishment.

In the light spectrum, green light received by plants is relatively unimportant for photosynthesis, which is a point noted later in connection with artificial lighting to take the place of sunlight. Blue light has some importance, and recent experiments in Germany have shown that to some extent blue light at a high intensity can substitute for part of red light. Red light has been found to have a vital effect on such important phases as seed germination, stem growth and leaf expansion. And very red, farther along the spectrum from red, works in a precise balance with red light, and must be present also for normal growth.

These points about the effect on plants of different colors of the light spectrum are important when plants are grown indoors, in rooms without sunlight. The use of incandescent light for the plants has the negative point of generating heat. Cool white lamps are high enough in the green-light area to reduce plant growth. The fluorescent lamps made especially for use with plants, though avoiding excessive green light, retain ultraviolet light which is also growth-inhibiting.

Fluorescent light is being used in various ways by indoor gardeners: in banks of tubes, square panels and circular units. Suggestions for meeting the needs of a balanced supply of blue, red and very red light are found in Dr. Klein's article on this subject, listed in the bibliography.

At this time, combinations of incandescent and fluorescent lamps offer the best answer to growing plants indoors. For intensity or quantity of light, Dr. Klein suggests 30 to 40 watts per square foot. The duration of lighting, whether sunlight or artificial, depends to some extent on the type of plant, which can be noted in its culture directions. Also when artificial light is used, the timing depends on whether the artificial light supplements sunlight or provides all the appreciable light. In the latter case, the average plant could have ten hours of light a day for sturdy growth and good bloom.

Meanwhile research work goes on. This means not only the advance of theory concerning the relationship of light and plants, but also the practical application of new knowledge to the improvement of lighting for plants in the house.

High in importance for the future is the possible use of plants on space flights. Plants can be valuable in restoring oxygen to the confined area of a space vehicle during a trip. Some waste products of men and animals may be used by the plants to stimulate their growth. And plants may be vital for food on long trips to distant planets.

Some algae, yeasts, and some of the fungi are considered possible sources. Research is being done on their uses for food on long flights.

Yeast plants not only are a good source of protein and other nutrients, but they multiply swiftly. This speed, of course, would be important on a space flight, compared to slower growth of other plants. Yeasts can utilize animal wastes, thus performing another service on the way to producing protein.

Though algae can't be used as food for human beings on long space voyages, they have an important part to play here on earth, as discussed below. They can be a valuable weapon against the famine that attacks many countries. Yeasts have their value, and some forms of fungi are a source of protein. But the most interesting possibilities, at present, are offered by algae.

Algae are plants that grow in water. They grow fast, their cells absorbing chemicals, as other plants do, and producing proteins, carbohydrates and vitamins.

Their food values have been known for a long time. They have been cultivated for centuries in shallow waters of the Sea of Japan, for food.

Their culture and possibilities for their wider utilization as food are discussed by Hiroshi Tamiya, in his paper on the "Role of Algae as Food," listed in the bibliography. About twenty different kinds of algae are used for food in Japan. The most popular, sold under the name of "Asakusa-Nori," is made of Rhodophyceae, *Porphyra tenera,* which is cultivated in shallow seas. The annual amount of this product of ocean farms totals as much as 400 to 500 metric tons, dry weight.

In this algal farming, beds are laid on the sea bottom. The most primitive method is of erecting leafless brush-bamboo and brushwood of other sorts on the seabed, with their tops reaching the level of high tide, to keep the algae from drifting away. A more sophisticated method is the net bed, using nets a hundred and twenty feet long, spread across bamboo rods on the sea bottom.

Young algae are started in the beds and tended as they grow. Professor Tamiya describes their harvesting: small boats float along alleys in the algae beds, on points of the seacoast around Japan, while the algal farmers pluck pieces of algae by hand and pile them in baskets.

After harvesting, they are processed by being washed in fresh water, cut into small pieces, and spread on *sunokos,* or filter plates, to dry. When dry, the algal sheets are stripped off the *sunokos* and sent to market.

Before they are eaten, the algal sheets are usually toasted over a slow fire. This improves the taste, as well as giving a crisp texture. The toasted algal sheet is eaten with rice, vegetables and other kinds of food.

Various methods are now being considered to increase the crop of algae. A future possibility is growing algae in tanks instead of the sea, as Japanese coastal sites are limited.

This form of algae has been grown in mass and used as food in Japan for some centuries. Another genus of algae, *Chlorella,* has been studied for the past decade. This form can grow in a wide range of temperatures. Most of the *Chlorella* species studied so far live in fresh water.

Chlorella is distributed widely through many countries, and thus its adoption as food in countries threatened by famine is readily possible. It is unusually rich in proteins and vitamins.

A pilot plant has been built in Japan, to test the feasibility of producing *Chlorella* on an industrial scale. Estimates are being made, in this country as well as in Japan, of mass production costs for growing the alga. Algal farming, for other countries that have not yet tried it, seems only a step ahead in the future.

New food plants, or those new to some countries, are already appearing here and there around the world. Some of these are fairly new to this country.

We may be hearing more of the Chinese gooseberry in the United States, for example. The juice of these berries is over fifteen times richer in vitamin C than orange juice. Chinese gooseberries have been used in New Zealand and are now appearing in parts of the United States.

Also in the future, we may make better use of plants already familiar here. The elderberry is one of our native plants, and is also a rich source of vitamin C. Elderberry jelly, an old-time favorite, may make a comeback. Then there are wild-mustard leaves for the tossed salad, full of vitamins and trace minerals that are important in nutrition. And sunflower seeds, appreciated in Russia, India and Egypt, as well as by our wild birds, may come into vogue here when their food value is better known.

Research is bringing us wider knowledge about plants and their values for us, and this will continue. But an important part of plant performance in the future is tied to our own recognition of the need to guard our plants.

Plants are being destroyed, in widening stretches, through erosion, fire, urbanization and other enemies such as pests spread by man. Our natural resources are not limitless.

Ecology, the relationship between living organisms and their environments, is a vital part of the future for us. An understanding of ecology is absolutely necessary to our future management of all natural resources, including plants.

We will have to give back something more, to the plants from which we take so much, to protect our own future needs. A partnership is vitally needed here. Without it, neither men nor our plants can survive.

Where to Buy Seeds and Plants

Seeds, bulbs, seedlings and plants, as well as flowerpots, potting-soil mixtures, and plant-growth stimulators or inhibitors, may be purchased at many plant nurseries and hardware stores. Unusual varieties of plants can be ordered by mail from a number of suppliers throughout the country, some of which are listed below.

The Pearce Seed Company
Moorestown, New Jersey 08057

White Flower Farm
Litchfield, Connecticut 06759

George W. Park Seed Company
Greenwood, South Carolina 29646

Jackson & Perkins
Newark, New York 14513

The Wayside Gardens
Mentor, Ohio 44060

W. G. Burpee Seed Company
Riverside, California 92502

Bibliography

Technical sources and scientific papers are listed below, along with books of general interest for the average reader. The latter are marked with an asterisk.

Alvord, Benjamin, "On the Compass Plant." *American Naturalist,* Vol. XVI, August, 1882.

Audus, L. J., "Magnotropism: A New Plant Growth Response." London, *Nature,* Vol. 185, 1960.

Baker, John R., "A Floral Clock." *Royal Horticultural Society Journal,* Vol. 65, 1940.

Brown, O. A., Stone, R. B., Jr., and Andrews, Henry, "Methods and Equipment for Low Energy Irradiation of Seeds." *Agricultural Engineering,* September, 1957.

Bünning, Erwin, *The Physiological Clock.* New York, Springer-Verlag, 1967.

* Carson, Rachel, *Silent Spring.* Boston, Houghton Mifflin Company, 1962.

Chute, Willard N., "Plant Partnerships." *Gardeners' Chronicle,* March, 1921.

* Cooper, Elizabeth K., *Insects and Plants: The Amazing Partnership.* New York, Harcourt, Brace & World, Inc., 1963.

Daglish, E. Fitch, *Marvels of Plant Life.* London, Thornton Butterworth, Ltd., 1924.

Darwin, Charles, *The Power of Movement in Plants.* New York, D. Appleton & Company, Inc., 1896.

Dolk, Herman E., "Movements of Leaves of the Compass-plant *Lac-*

tuca Scariola." *American Journal of Botany,* Vol. XVIII, March, 1931.

Dyer, H. J., ed., "Response to Ultrasound: Plants." The Federation of American Societies for Experimental Biology, 1966.

———, and Nyborg, W. L., "Characteristics of Intracellular Motion Induced by Ultrasound." London, *Proceedings of the Third International Conference on Medical Electronics,* 1960.

———, "Ultrasonically-Induced Movements in Cells and Cell Models." *IRE Transactions on Medical Electronics,* Vol. ME-7, July, 1960.

* Gibbons, Euell, *Stalking the Wild Asparagus.* New York, David McKay Company, Inc., 1962.

Gürwitsch, Alexander, "Radiation and Life." *Harpers,* July, 1934.

* Hutchins, Ross E., *Strange Plants and Their Ways.* Chicago, Rand McNally and Company, 1958.

* Hyde, Margaret, *Plants Today and Tomorrow.* New York, McGraw-Hill Book Co., Inc., 1960.

Jaffe, M. J., and Galston, A. W., "Physiological Studies on Pea Tendrils: I. Growth and Coiling Following Mechanical Stimulation." *Plant Physiology,* Vol. 41, June, 1967.

* Kavaler, Lucy, *Mushrooms, Molds, and Miracles: The Strange Realm of Fungi.* New York, The John Day Company, 1965.

Kenly, Julie C., *Green Magic: The Story of the World of Plants.* New York, D. Appleton & Company, 1930.

* Klein, H. Arthur, *Bioluminescence.* Philadelphia, J. B. Lippincott Company, 1965.

Klein, Richard M., "On the Reported Effects of Sound on the Growth of Plants." *BioScience,* February, 1965.

———, "Packaged Sunshine." *The Garden Journal,* July–August, 1966.

* ———, and Klein, Deana T., *Discovering Plants.* New York, The Natural History Press, 1968.

Krylor, A. V. and Tarakanova, "Magnetism Affects Plants." *Science News Letter,* July 23, 1960.

Lasagna, Louis, *The Doctors' Dilemmas.* New York, Collier Books, 1963.

Monahan, N. F., "The Influence of the Atmospherical Electrical Potential on Plants." *Annual Report of the Hatch Experiment Station of the Massachusetts Agricultural College, 1904.*

————, "The Influence of the Electrical Potential on the Growth of Plants." *Annual Report of the Hatch Experiment Station of the Massachusetts Agricultural College, 1905.*

* Parker, Bertha M., *Seeds and Seed Travels.* New York, Harper & Brothers, 1941.

Philbrick, Helen, and Gregg, Richard, *Companion Plants and How to Use Them.* New York, The Devin-Adair Company, 1966.

* Selsam, Millicent, *Plants That Move.* New York, William Morrow & Company, Inc., 1962.

Stefferud, Alfred, *The Wonders of Seeds.* New York, Harcourt, Brace, & Co., Inc., 1956.

Stone, G. E., "The Influence of Current Electricity on Plant Growth." *Annual Report of the Hatch Experiment Station of the Massachusetts Agricultural College, 1904.*

Tamiya, Hiroshi, "Role of Algae as Food." *Proceedings of the Symposium on Algology,* New Delhi, 1959.

* Verrill, A. Hyatt, *Wonder Plants and Plant Wonders.* New York, D. Appleton-Century Company, Inc., 1939.

Warner, Anne S., *Effects of Electricity on the Germination of Seeds.* Unpublished M.S. thesis, University of Massachusetts, 1967.

Weintraub, Marvin, "Leaf Movements in *Mimosa pudica.*" *New Phytologist,* Vol. 50, January, 1952.

Index

[*Page numbers in italics denote illustrations.*]

cobalt 60, 66–68
cobra lily, 30
cold and plant life, 69–71
Columbia University, 70
compass plant, 8, *9*
corn seeds, 57
cotton seeds, 42
cottonwood tree, 42
cryogenics, 70–71
curare, 75

Daglish, E. Fitch, 50
daisies, African, 13
dandelion, 13, 42
dandelion puffball, 24
Darwin, Charles, 11, 19, 20
day lilies, 13
Desmodium canadense, 45
Desmodium gyrans, 10
Dictamnus albus, 10
digitalis, 73
dinoflagellates, 51
dock (herb), 72
dwarfing of plants, 18, 23, 69
Dyer, Dr. Hubert J., 63

ecology, 87
elderberry, 86
electricity, plants' responses to, 19, 24
electroculture, 53–61
ephedrine, 73
epinasty, 81
ethylene gas, 81, 82
evening primrose, 13
experiments, reporting of, 58–61

Federation of American Societies for Experimental Biology, 63
fireweed, 42
flies, 36
floral clock, 12
flowering plants in garden, 39

flowering tobacco, 13
flowerpots, 7, 8, 23, 26
  hanging, 11
flowers, 7, 12–13, 35, 49–51, 53, 55, 56, 67
  freezing of, 69–71
four-o'clocks, 13
foxglove, 73
freezing of flowers and seeds, 69–71
Fry, Dr., 56–57
Fukada, E., 58
fungus, 38, 50, 51, 70, 78, 80, 84

Galston, Dr. A. W., 21
Gardener's Chronicle of 1859, 50
gardenias, 55
gardens:
  ancient, 7
  atomic, 65–68
  experiments in, 20–24, 55, 56, 58–61
  indoor, 7, 8, 11, 25–26, 83
  luminescence in, 51–52
  on Mars, 78, 79
  of performing plants, 7–16
  vegetable, 39, 53
  of walking plants, 14
garlic, 33, 72
gas plant (*Dictamnus albus*), 10
Gates, H. E., 45
gentians, 13
geotropism, 18
geraniums, 17, 23
gesnerads, 41–42, 70
giant plants, 18, 23
gibberellin (*Gibberella fujikuroi*), 80, 81
gladiolus, 18
goatsbeard, 13
Goethe, Johann Wolfgang von, 50, 52
goldenrod, 42